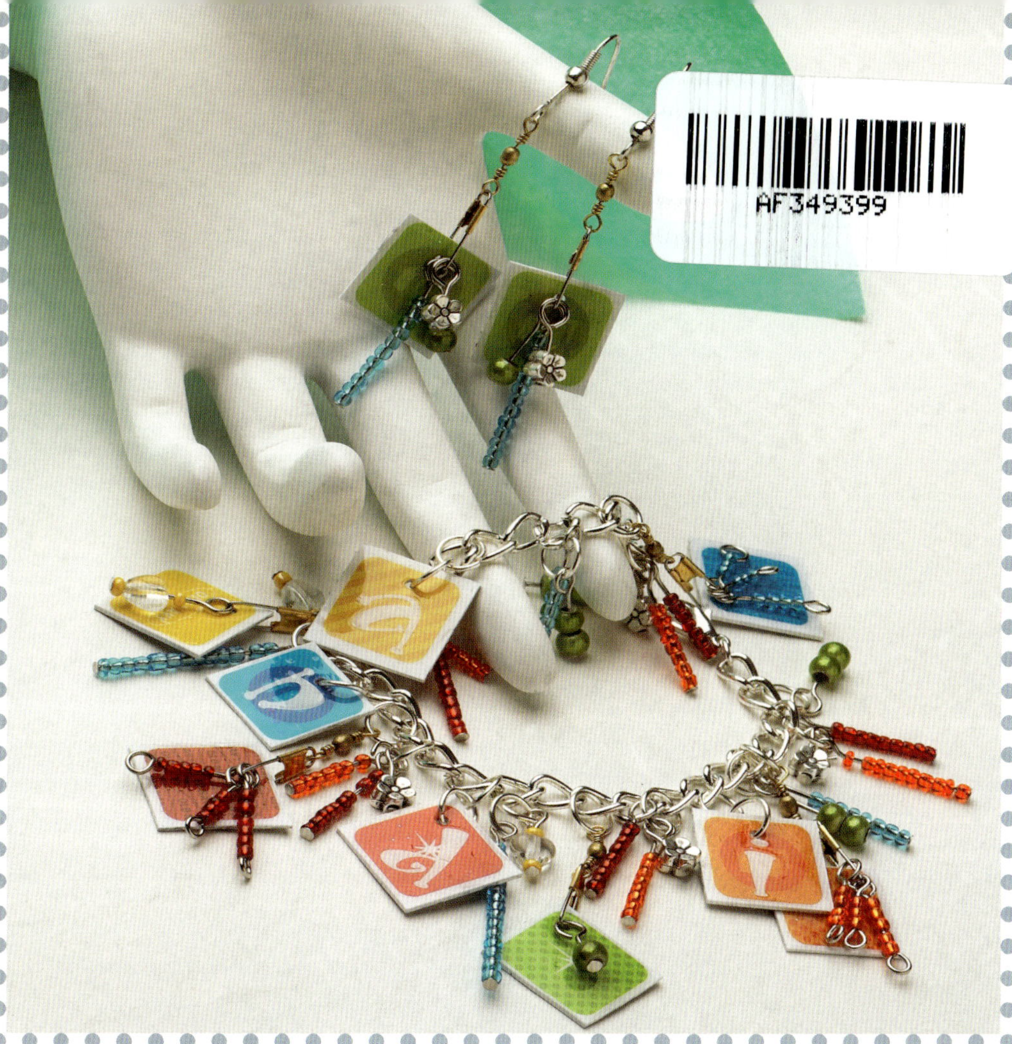

Measure and cut squares from a gift card.

Transfer rub-on letters onto squares with a smooth rubbing stick.

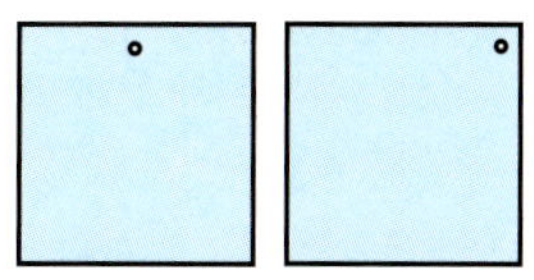

Punch a hole in each square, some in the center, some to the side.

Colorful Initial Bracelet and Earrings
by Andrea Gibson

Rub-on letters make it so easy to display your name, initials or a message on this colorful bracelet.

MATERIALS:
Gift card • Seed beads (60 Red, 80 Blue, 40 Orange, 10 Yellow) • Beads (11 small round Green, 3 small clear heart) • 7 Silver flower spacer beads • 5 size 14 snap swivel brass hooks • Silver non-tarnish 20 gauge wire • 25 medium Silver jump rings • 7" Silver charm bracelet • Earring wires • Eye pins • Head pins • Rub-on letters • Silver paint pen • 1/16" hole punch • Glossy Accents glaze

INSTRUCTIONS:
Gift Card Preparation: Cut card into 11 squares 3/4". Paint backs with Silver pen. Punch holes into each square. Rub-on letters. Glaze. Let dry.
Bead Dangles: Using head pins, make 6 Blue, 5 Red, and 5 Orange seed bead dangles. Close with a loop. • Using head pins, make 7 bead dangles with small round Green beads, 4 with 2 beads, 3 with 1 bead. Close with a loop. • Using head pins, make 7 bead dangles with flower spacers. Close with a loop. • Using head pins, make 3 bead dangles using 2 Yellow seed beads and 1 clear heart. Close with a loop. • Using 9 eye pins, load 4-5 seed beads each to make 3 Blue, 3 Red, and 3 Orange bead dangles.
Bracelet Assembly: Cluster bead dangles as listed, attaching to bracelet with medium jump rings. Left to Right: Green; Red-Orange-flower; Swivel hook-square-3 small Blue bead strands; Green-Blue strand; square; Red-Orange-flower; swivel hook-square-heart; Blue strand-heart, square; swivel hook-square-3 small Red strands; Red-Orange-flower; square; Blue-heart; swivel hook-square-Green; Red-Orange-flower; square; Green-Blue strand; swivel hook-square-3 small Orange bead strands; Red-Orange-flower; Green.
Earrings: Load swivel hook with long Blue strand, Green bead, flower and square. Attach to earring wire.

Basic Steps

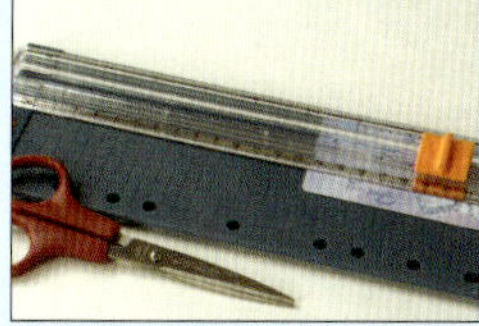

1. Use scissors or a paper trimmer to cut gift cards.

2. Use a hand punch, shaped punch or Sizzix to cut shapes.

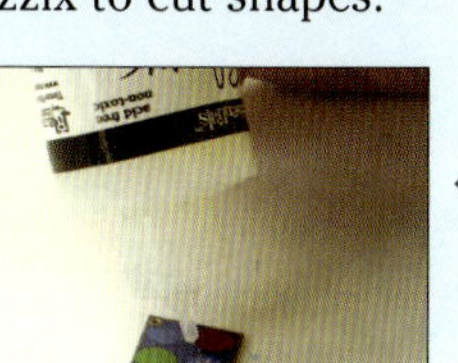

3. Apply Glossy Accents.

4. Use rub-ons to add initials, names or accents.

5. Set eyelets for a finished look.

6. Use pliers to bend wires to connect bead dangles and cards.

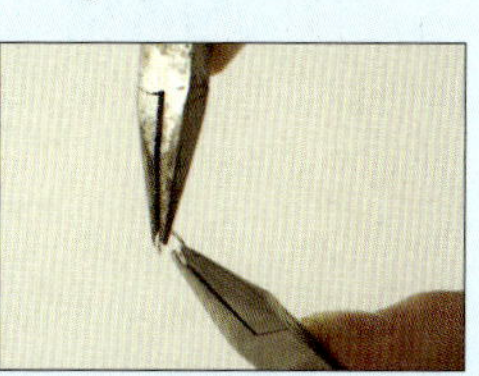

7. Use pliers to twist jump rings open and closed.

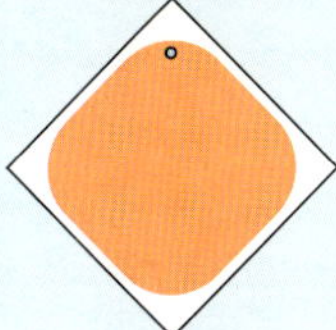

Basic Wire Techniques:

Special Note:

Working with wire is an awesome way to customize your jewelry. These basic techniques make working with wire creative, flexible and oh so fun. With a little wire, some basic tools and your creativity, you can make a beautiful project to be worn and admired by everyone. These wire techniques can be adapted in many other projects from jewelry to scrapbooking and cardmaking and even home craft projects. I hope you enjoy wire as much as I do.

Coil and Jump Rings Use Wire Worker System or a dowel to get a nice smooth coil. Dowels come in different sizes, choose three sizes for the projects in this book - Small 1/8", Medium 3/16", and Large 1/4".

Wrap wire on a wire worker or on a dowel tightly to form a tight coil. If need be, you can push coils together to get a tight coil. Remove coil from wire worker or dowel, cutting off ends, flush with your coil.

To make jump rings, pull coil slightly apart and cut each loop with wire cutters. I like to hold the coil in the palm of my hand, place the wire cutters in the middle of my coil and cut. You get a few jump rings at a time. Remember when using jump rings, you need to slide open and closed. Do not bend outwards to open as this will ruin your jump ring, not allowing it to close tightly. To get a secure hold when using jump rings, use 18 or 20 gauge wire.

Loop: Hold the end of the wire with round-nose pliers; make turn counterclockwise until end meets main wire – forming a small circle. This forms a perfect loop every time.

S-Hooks: Use round-nose pliers to turn a loop in one end of the wire. Turn another loop in opposite direction at the other end of the wire. Each S-hook takes about 1" of wire.

Loop Bead Units: Use round-nose pliers to turn a loop in one end of wire. Thread bead or beads and turn another loop to complete loop bead unit. Each bead unit uses 1"-2" of wire depending on bead size.

Wrap Bead Units: Wrap bead units are stronger than loop bead units.

Use round-nose pliers to bend down 1" of wire – about a fingers width. Roll into a loop. While holding loop on round-nose pliers tightly, closely wrap short end around long end 3 to 4 times. Trim excess with wire cutters. Load beads onto long wire. Repeat bead wrap steps at open end to complete wrap bead unit. Make sure to leave space beyond last bead for wrapping wire. Trim wire. Each wrap bead unit used 2"-4" of wire depending on loaded bead size.

Swirl: Begin each swirl with a tiny loop in the end of the wire. Using flat-nose pliers or nylon jaw pliers, grasp the loop, swirling or gently turning the loop around and around to make your swirl. This can be done tightly or loosely depending on the look you desire. Tip: I find it very easy to turn a swirl with my hands by placing the loop between my thumb and index finger and turning clockwise. If your swirl is not as flat as you would like, use a hammer or nylon jaw pliers to flatten.

Bent Swirl Dangles: Close top of dangle with a loop. Shape and bend wire with round-nose pliers, adding beads is optional. Bend loop in bottom of wire and make swirl to desired size to close dangle. There are endless configurations to bent swirl dangles. Each dangle uses 2"-4" of wire.

Spiral Wire Beads: Using the smallest wire worker or dowel, coil wire loosely. Remove wire by sliding off dowel. Turn loop in one end and flatten with flat nose pliers or nylon jaw pliers. Tip: Coil a long spiral piece. Cut several spiral beads from one coil.

Fancy Lady Pin

by Andrea Gibson

If unique is what you seek, the Fancy Lady pin is for you. When everyone asks where you bought this designer pin, you'll be proud to proclaim, "I made it myself!"

SIZE: 2 1/4" x 3 3/4"

MATERIALS:

Flower shaped gift card • Seed beads (Pink, Violet) • 1 1/4" pin back • Metal dragonfly spacer bead • Polymer face shape • Silver non-tarnish wire: 20 and 22 gauge • 2 medium jump rings • *Krylon* Black fusion spray paint for plastic • Sanding block • 1/16" hole punch • GLOO Clear adhesive

INSTRUCTIONS:

Card Preparation: Paint back of card Black. Let dry. Cut card into 2 different sized pieces. Round edges if desired. Sand all edges. Punch 10 holes. See diagram on page 5.

Card Assembly: Glue face in place. Cut 10" of 22 gauge wire. Leaving a 1/4" gap between cards, lace cards together diagonally, adding Pink and Violet seed beads in a random pattern and dragonfly. Finish wire end with a loose swirl. Using 16" of 22 gauge wire, wrap pin. Begin with a loose swirl, wrap top to bottom, add beads randomly, finish wrap with a swirl on front of pin.

Shaped Swirl Dangles: Using 20 gauge wire, cut 5" and two 3" lengths. Shape swirl dangles following pattern, making a loop at top of design for attachment to pin. Use 2 medium jump rings to dangle from the bottom corner. Glue the pin back in place.

Live in the Sunshine Pin

by Andrea Gibson

Round windows add interest and dimension to this bright as sunshine pin.

Tip: Line up both card designs before cutting cards, making sure design will show through windows for added dimensional look.

SIZE: 1 3/4" x 2 3/4"

MATERIALS:

2 gift cards • Pink brad • 1 1/4" pin back • Flower sequins • 2 round, Pink metal frames • Transparency Film • Snap Swivel size 14 Brass hooks • *Krylon* Black Fusion spray paint for plastic • StazOn Jet Black ink • Punches (Corner rounder, Circles: 1/16", 1") • Black foam adhesive strips

INSTRUCTIONS:

Gift Card Preparation: Computer print "Live in the Sunshine" on transparency film, making sure to space words with circle windows punched in card. • Paint backs of both gift cards with Black. Cut cards 1 3/4" x 2 3/4", being careful to cut the exact card area from both cards so that once assembled it is a duplicate image.

Top Card: Punch two 1" circles in gift card. Round corners. Ink edges. Glue printed transparency on back of card to show through windows. Add Pink frames to top of card. Punch hole in right bottom corner. Add flower sequins to snap swivel hook, attach to card with Pink brad. Add Black foam strips around edges, set aside.

Bottom Card: Ink edges. Lining up card designs, attach top to bottom card with foam strips.

Finish: Glue pin back in place.

1. Punch circles out of card.

2. Adhere transparency to card, trim.

3. Add Pink metal frames.

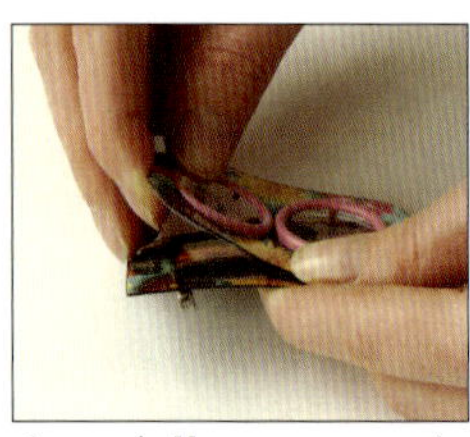

4. Adhere cards together with foam strips.

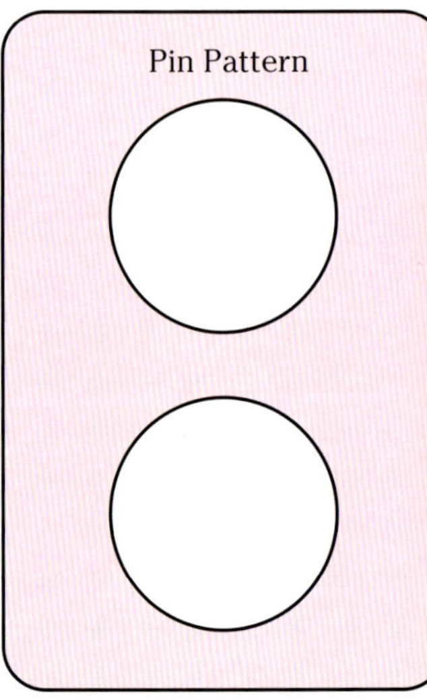

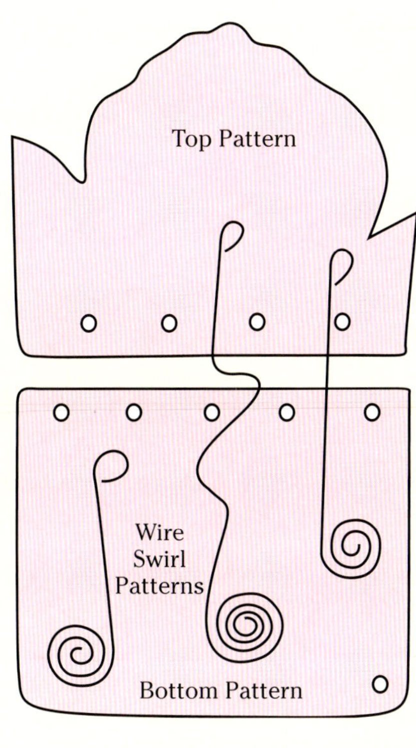

Top Pattern

Wire Swirl Patterns

Bottom Pattern

1. Cut card.

2. Punch holes in cards so holes are mismatched.

3. Lace cards together with wire, adding beads while lacing.

Groovy Dangle Earrings
by Andrea Gibson

Geometric shape gives these earrings a clean, stylish, look... very retro and very now!

Tip: If using a holographic card with tiny grooves, the ink may run a little. While this is a neat effect, test on a spare card piece prior to using ink on your project to gauge how much ink you want to use.

MATERIALS:
2 gift cards • Silver non-tarnish 20 gauge wire • Jump rings (6 medium, 4 large) • Earring wire • 2 Black Czech pressed dagger drops • Sequins (Pink, Green) • StazOn Blazing Red inkpad • Silver paint pen • Die cut machine, Squares die: 2 smallest patterns

INSTRUCTIONS:

Gift Card Preparation: From each card, diecut 1 medium and 1 smaller square. Sand outside edges of both square sets. Paint backs of all squares with Silver marker. Let dry. Ink outside edges with Blazing Red. Pierce hole in all pieces at one corner.
• Connect small square to large square with 1 large jump ring. Add a Green and a Pink sequin to jump ring before closing. • At bottom corner of large square, attach 2 Pink sequins with a large jump ring. Add another medium jump ring with 2 Pink sequins and 1 small Black dagger bead. • Use medium jump ring to connect earring wire at the top.

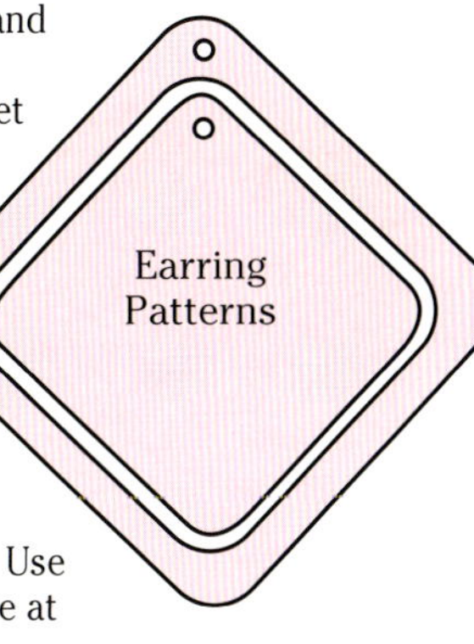

Earring Patterns

1. Die cut or punch out the squares.

2. Punch a hole in the corner.

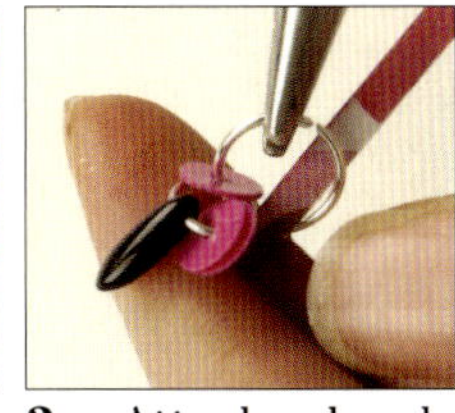

3. Attach dangle with a jump ring.

1. Apply Glossy Accents, add beads while wet. Add second coat over beads.

2. Add beads to swirl dangle, close with a loop.

Making a Loop Unit

1. Using round-nose pliers, bend ³⁄₈" of wire or head pin at a 90° angle.

2. Grasp wire end with round-nose pliers; roll down forming loop. Close loop completely after attaching it to item.

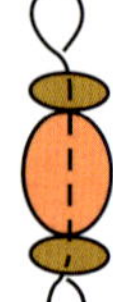

Peace Bracelet
by Andrea Gibson

Warm colors embrace your wrist and touch your spirit with tranquil beauty.

MATERIALS:
2 gift cards • Silver non-tarnish 20 gauge wire • Jump rings • Bead mix • 6 saucer beads • Oblong beads (5 large, 8 small) • Copper beads (50 seed, 10 rondelle 6mm) • Copper dragonfly charm • PEACE Brass charm word • 12mm Lobster Claw clasp • Silver paint pen • Sanding block • Circle punches (¹⁄₁₆", 1") • Glossy Accents • GLOO Clear adhesive

INSTRUCTIONS:

Card Preparation: Punch 4 circles from gift cards. Sand edges smooth. Paint back of each circle with Silver marker. Let dry. Punch hole in top of each circle. Glaze. While wet, add loose Copper seed beads to 3 circles, 8-10 each. Add word charm to remaining circle. After first coat of glaze dries on all beads, glaze again and dry.

Loop Bead Units: Cut fifteen 3" pieces of Silver wire. Make 15 loop bead units with multiple bead and color combinations. Loop bead units will vary in size according to bead combinations.

Swirl Dangles: Cut four 2" pieces of Silver wire. Turn a loop in top, add 6 Copper seed beads. Close by making a small swirl in the end.

Bracelet Assembly: Link 7 of the larger loop bead units together to form bracelet, checking wrist size. • Add 1 medium jump ring and lobster claw clasp to one end. Link together 6 medium jump rings, add to other end for bracelet sizing. Dangle 2 small loop bead units and dragonfly charm from end of jump rings. • To complete bracelet, attach 4 circles to 4 loop bead units with medium jump rings. Space evenly and attach to bracelet with medium jump rings. In between circles, group and attach 2 swirl dangles and a loop bead unit with a medium jump ring.

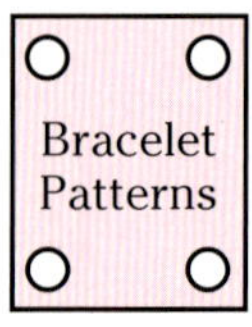

Rectangles Bracelet
by Michele Charles

Capture the romance of flowers in a bracelet that is perfect for dressing up your favorite summer frock.

MATERIALS: Gift card • Gold clasp • Gold jump rings (3mm, 5mm) • Tiny eyelets • ¹⁄₁₆" hole punch • Eyelet tools

INSTRUCTIONS:

Gift Card Preparation: Cut card into 6 rectangles ⁵⁄₈" x ³⁄₄" and 2 strips ¹⁄₈" x ⁵⁄₈". Punch holes following diagram. Set eyelets.

Bracelet: Put a 5mm jump ring in each hole. Connect 3mm jump rings to 5mm jump rings. Attach clasp.

1. Measure rectangles ⁵⁄₈" x ³⁄₄"

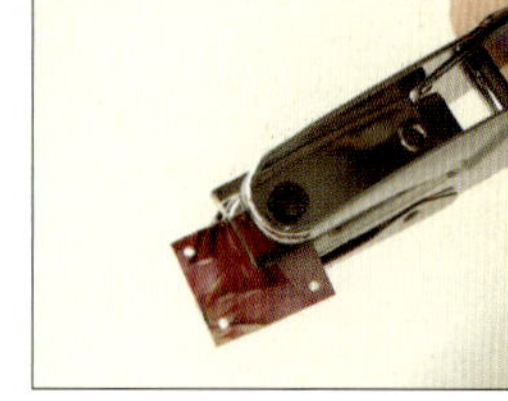

2. Cut rectangles.

3. Punch ¹⁄₁₆" holes in rectangle.

4. Set an eyelet in each hole.

5. Connect rectangles with jump rings.

Happy Heart Key Fob
by Andrea Gibson

Collage lovers, this key fob will tickle your fancy and make your creative heart happy with its bright colors and artsy design.

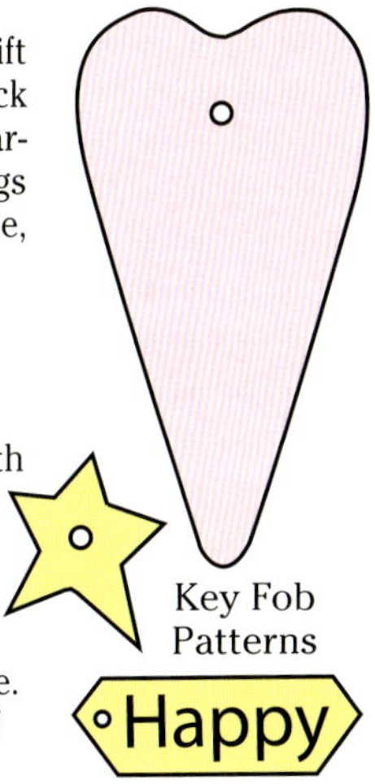

MATERIALS:
Gift card • "Happy" words cut from gift card • Key ring square • 5 small Black beads • Sunshine charm • Silver non-tarnish 20 gauge wire • 4 small jump rings • Silver paint pen • Die cut machine, Dies: Primitive heart, Primitive star • 1/16" hole punch

INSTRUCTIONS:
Gift Card Preparation: Die cut heart and star from gift card. Paint backs with Silver marker. Punch hole in top of heart and star.
Loop bead units: Make 3 loop bead units with Black beads.
Happy Heart Assembly: Cut 9" of wire. Thread 3" of wire from back to front of heart. Add star. Make swirl in end of wire, loosely zigzag, bend flat in place. Bend remaining long wire from back of heart over right heart hump, then back up, bending into an upside down "v". Add 2 Black beads and 2 small jump rings to wire. Bend behind left heart hump, bend to front of heart following zigzag lines from other wire piece. Bend to back again and over to right side at base of heart. Make a wrapped loop at the end. Attach loop bead units to the end of wrapped loop. Dangle sunshine charm and "Happy" word from 1 bead unit. Attach heart to key ring with 2 small jump rings.

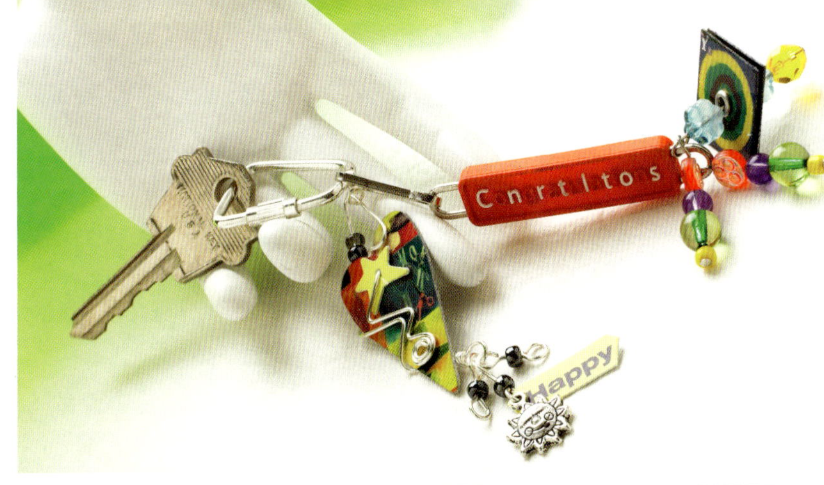

1. Bend wire into dip of heart, secure in front.

2. Bend wire back to front to match zigzag.

3. Add the dangle with a jump ring.

Bead Bracelet and Earrings
by Donna Goss

Gift cards with squares or circles on them are perfect for this project.

SIZE: 8 1/8"
MATERIALS:
2 gift cards • Toggle clasp • Tiger tail wire • Crimp beads • Silver eyelets • Head pins • Ear wires • Beads • Eggplant alcohol ink • Alcohol ink applicator • Non-stick craft sheet • Eyelet tools • Crimping pliers • Tweezers • 1/8" hole punch

INSTRUCTIONS:
Gift Card beads: Cut gift card into 3/4" squares, 6 for bracelet, 4 for earrings. Apply alcohol ink to backs and sides of squares. Punch a hole in the center of each square. Set an eyelet in each hole.
Bracelet: Cut 12" of tiger tail wire. Thread crimp bead and 1 end of clasp onto wire. Thread end of wire back through crimp bead. Crimp. • Thread beads and gift card squares on wire in a pleasing pattern. Place bracelet around wrist to measure length. Add beads until it is the correct size. Thread crimp bead, then other end of toggle clasp on wire. Thread end of wire back through crimp bead and the last 3 beads. Pull tight and remove slack from bracelet. Crimp. Trim wire if needed.
Earrings: On headpin, slide beads and squares with alcohol ink backs touching. Slide on more beads. Trim head pin 1/4" from last bead. Make a loop and attach to earring loop base before closing.

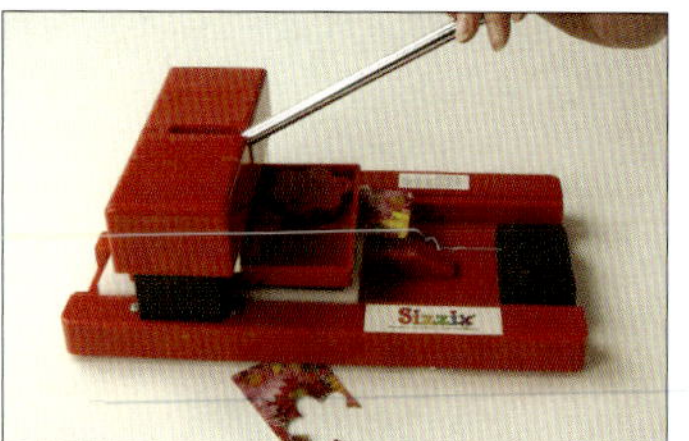

1. Die cut flower shape.

2. Melt glue onto back of jewel with BeJeweler.

3. Adhere crystals to flower with BeJeweler.

Rhinestone Flower Pin

by Donna Goss

Use this colorful item as a pin or a necklace on your favorite blouse.

SIZE: 3¹/₂"

MATERIALS:

Gift card • Heart charm • Pin bail back • 3mm crystals • Silver eyelet • 2 head pins • 2 jump rings • Beads • Silver paint pen • Eyelet tools • BeJeweler Stone Styler • Die cut machine, Flower die • ¹/₈" hole punch • Adhesive

INSTRUCTIONS:

Flower shape: Die cut flower shape from gift card. Paint edges and back. Let dry. Punch hole in one petal. Set eyelet. Attach crystals to center of flower with BeJeweler.

Bead dangles: Thread beads on head pin. Trim head pin ¹/₄" from last bead. Make a loop in wire and close near last bead.

Pin: Attach bead dangles to flower with jump ring. Attach heart charm to jump ring with the other jump ring. Glue pin bail back in place.

Stamp flower with StazOn ink.

Flower Necklace

by Donna Goss

Feeling tropical? Punch up your wardrobe all year around with a flower necklace in lush colors.

SIZE: 30"

MATERIALS:

3 gift cards • 30" chain necklace • Clipolas • Love word charms • Silver eyelets • Head pins • Jump rings • Beads • *A Stamp in the Hand* Word stamp • Cranberry alcohol ink • Alcohol ink applicator • Non-stick craft sheet • Jet Black StazOn inkpad • Eyelet tools • Die cut machine, Flower die • ¹/₈" hole punch

INSTRUCTIONS:

Flower shapes: Die cut 3 flower shapes. Cover the backs with alcohol ink. Stamp words on front and back of flowers. Punch hole in one petal on each flower. Set eyelet.

Bead dangles: Thread beads on head pin. Trim head pin ¹/₄" from last bead. Make a loop in wire and close near last bead.

Necklace: Apply alcohol ink to back of love word charms. Attach flowers, clipolas, charms, and beads dangles to chain with jump rings.

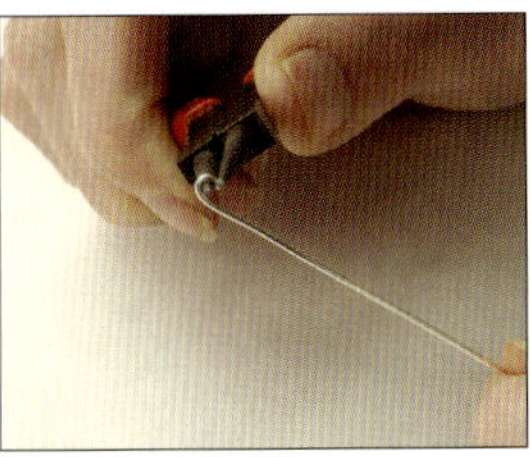

Making a Swirl

1. Use round-nose pliers to begin wire swirl with a loop.

2. Use flat-nose pliers to turn and continue swirl.

3. Use round-nose pliers to make a loop in the opposite end.

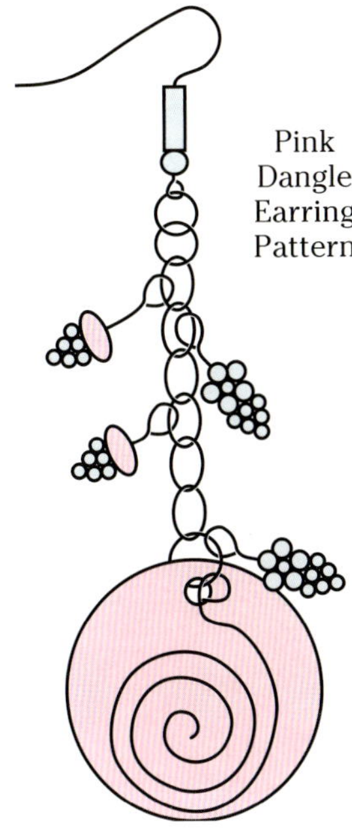

Dangle Earrings
by Andrea Gibson

You'll love the weightless sparkle of these pretty dangles.

SIZE: 1 1/2"
MATERIALS:
2 gift cards • Beads (4 Pink faceted rondelles, 4 Silver flower spacers) • 8 decorative head pins • Earring wire • 2 Silver 2" lengths of large wide cable chain • Silver non-tarnish 20 gauge wire • Jump rings (4 small, 2 medium) • Silver paint pen • Sanding block • Circle punches (1/16", 1")
INSTRUCTIONS:
Gift Card Preparation: Punch 2 identical circles from 2 gift cards. Paint back of circle with Silver paint pen. Sand edges smooth. Punch a hole in top of circle.
Loop Bead Units: Using decorative head pins, make 4 loop units with Silver flower beads and 4 loop units with Pink rondelle beads. See page 6.
Shape Loose Swirls: Cut two 6" Silver wires and shape into loose swirl. At end of swirl, turn a loop to attach swirl to earring.
Earring Assembly: Attach loop bead units randomly to chain by loop. Attach 2 small jump rings to top of chain, add earring wire. Load medium jump ring with gift card circle, shaped swirl and 1 flower loop bead unit. Attach to bottom of chain.

Heart and Hand Pin
by Donna Goss

Cutting up a gift card creates a myriad of designs. This heart pin gets its brilliant starburst effect from a flower gift card.

SIZE: 2 1/2" x 4"
MATERIALS:
2 gift cards • Hand charm • Pin back • Beads • Silver 20 gauge wire • Glossy Accents • Non-stick craft sheet • Silver paint pen • Die cut machine, Heart die • 1/8" hole punch • Adhesive
INSTRUCTIONS:
Die cut a heart shape from each gift card. Use positive heart from one gift card and negative heart from other. Use the scissors to cut around negative one to help form heart frame. Use the paint pen on all edges and back side of each heart. Let dry. Punch hole in frame heart near top inside point. Cut a 2" piece of wire. Make a loop in one end with round-nose pliers. Thread on beads. Cut wire 1/4" up from last bead. Make a loop on end of wire. Add hand charm to one loop and attach the other loop to hole in heart frame. Glue frame heart to positive heart. Apply Glossy Accents to back of hearts. Let dry. Then apply it to front and let dry. Adhere pin back.

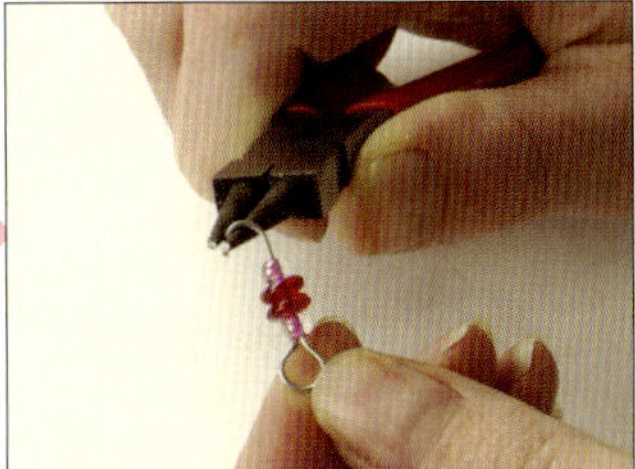

1. Make dangles.

2. Cut out around negative of heart.

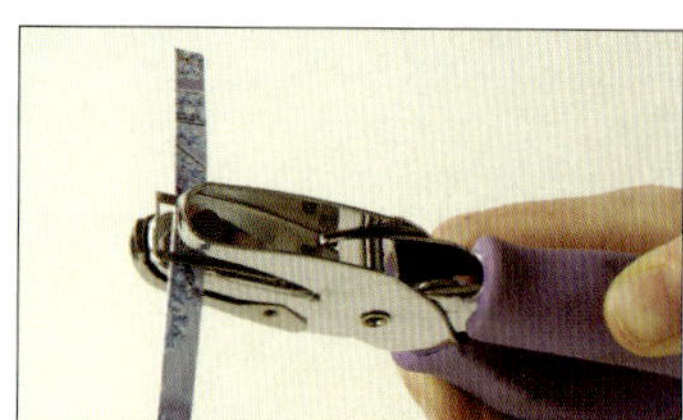

1. Punch a hole in the center of each strip.

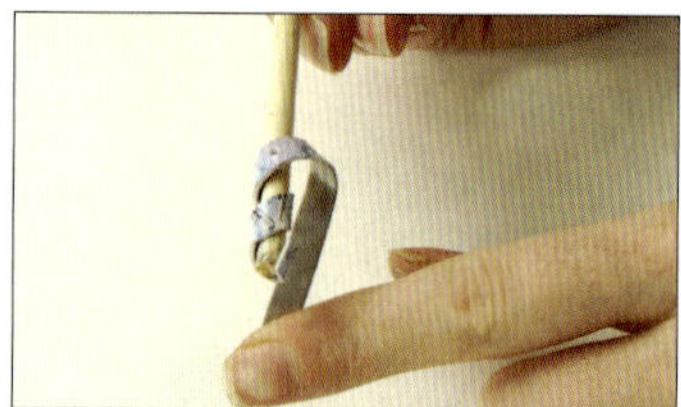

2. Wrap half of strip around dowel to form a spiral.

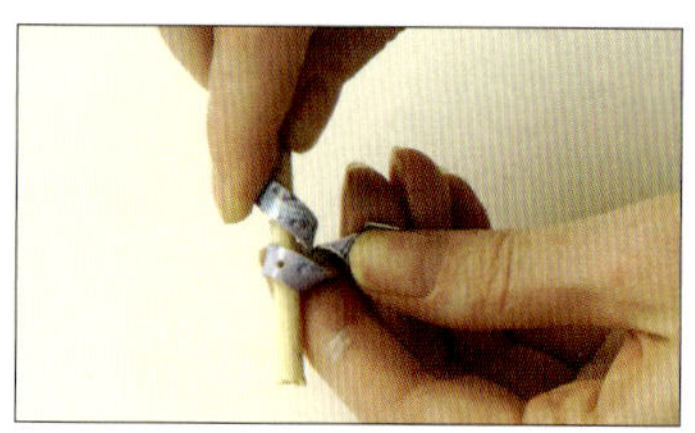

3. Flip and wrap the other side of strip around dowel.

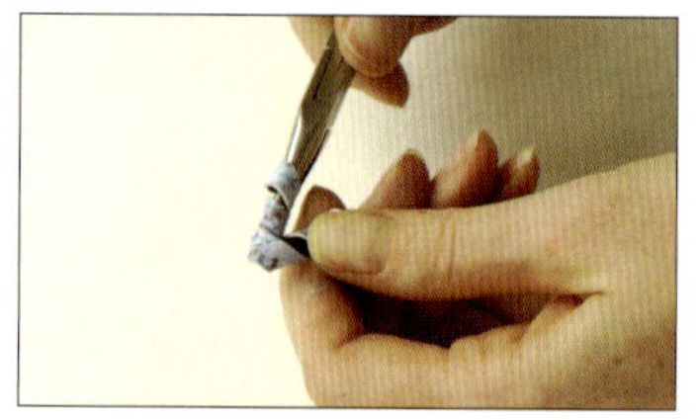

4. Shape spirals with pliers.

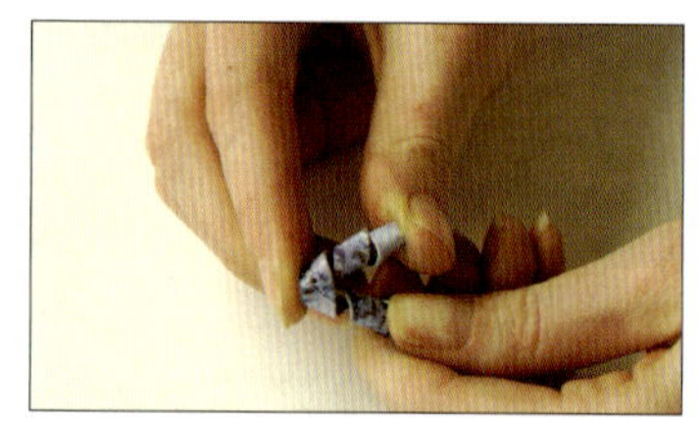

5. Tighten spirals by twisting.

Blue Curl Bracelet & Earrings
by Michele Charles

Whether you are feeling soft and quiet or outrageously bold, our Blue Curl bracelet is the perfect complement for your mood.

MATERIALS: Gift cards • Beads (13 Silver filigree 5mm, Silver lined E beads, Blue crystals, Blue seed beads) • Silver clasp • Beading wire • 2 Silver crimp beads • 2 ear wires • 13 Silver eye pins • 1/16" hole punch • Silver paint pen • 1/8" dowel rod
INSTRUCTIONS:
Gift Card Preparation: Cut cards in 1/4" strips. Punch hole in center of strip. Wrap one half of strip around dowel rod. Switch to other end and wrap around dowel. Shape ends with pliers. Tighten each curl by twisting tightly. Stretch each curl slightly.
Bracelet: Attach beading wire to 1 end of clasp with a crimp bead. Thread beads and eyepins onto wire. Attach other end of clasp to wire with a crimp bead. Thread eyepin with Silver bead. Curl end into a circle with round-nose pliers. Add E bead and curled strip to close circle.
Earrings: Punch hole in end of 2" strips. Curl around dowel. Attach to ear wires with beads.

Blue Key Fob
by Andrea Gibson

Give your keys, cards and baubles a new look with this fun key ring.

Tip: If using a holographic card with tiny grooves, the ink may run. While this is a neat effect, test on a spare piece of gift card prior to using ink on your project.

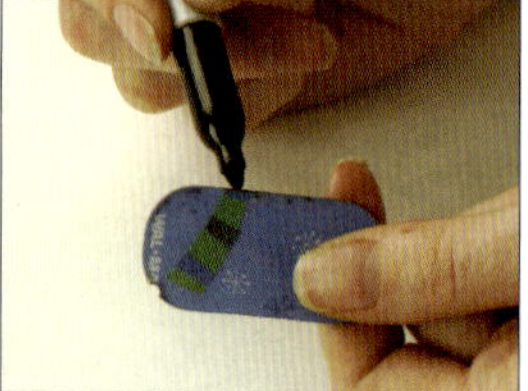

1. Cut out shape and ink edges.

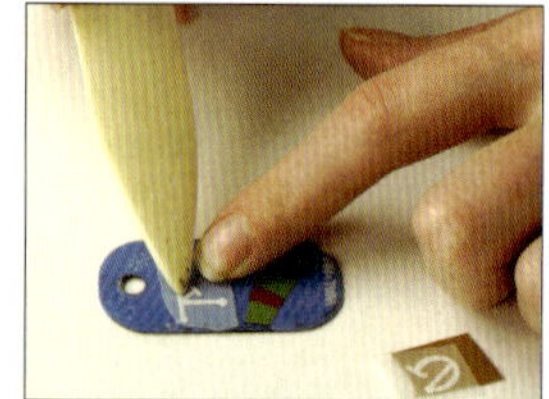

2. Transfer rub-on letters.

3. Punch hole in top.

4. Apply to key ring.

MATERIALS:
2 gift cards • Square key ring • 3 Blue and Pink bicone crystals • Alphabet beads • Metal flower • Blue ribbon • Silver non-tarnish 20 gauge wire • Rub-on letters • StazOn Jet Black inkpad • *Krylon* Black Fusion paint for plastic • Die cut machine, Dog Tag die • 1/4" hole punch
Gift Card Preparation: Paint back of cards Black. Die cut 1 tiny and 1 medium dog tag from same gift card. Cut 1 small dog tag from other gift card. Punch hole in each dog tag. Ink outside edges. Apply rub-on "KEYS" to medium dog tag. Load all tags onto key ring.
Bead Wrap: Cut 4" of wire. Make bead wrap with alphabet beads. Close bead wrap. Tie onto key ring with Blue ribbon. See page 16.
Loop Bead Units: Make 3 loop bead units with crystal beads. See page 6. Attach loops to end of alphabet bead wrap for extra dangle.

Multi Curl Bracelet

by Michele Charles

Irresistibly touchable, these curls are designed to be noticed!

SIZE: 9"

MATERIALS:

Gift cards • Gold beads • Assorted seed and round beads • Gold clasp • Beading wire • 2 Gold crimp beads • Gold jump rings (3mm, 5mm) • Twelve 3-prong fishing lures • Gold metallic paint pen • 1/8" dowel rod • 1/16" hole punch

INSTRUCTIONS:

Gift Card Preparation: Paint back of cards. Cut cards into 3/8" x 21/4" strip. Punch hole in one end. Curl around dowel rod. Shape ends with pliers. Twist to tighten. Attach a curl to each loop on fishing lure.

Bracelet: Attach 1 end of clasp to wire with a crimp bead. Thread Gold bead, lure, Gold bead, seed bead, round bead, seed bead. Repeat for length of bracelet. Attach end of wire to 3 mm jump ring. Attach 5mm jump ring to 3mm jump ring.

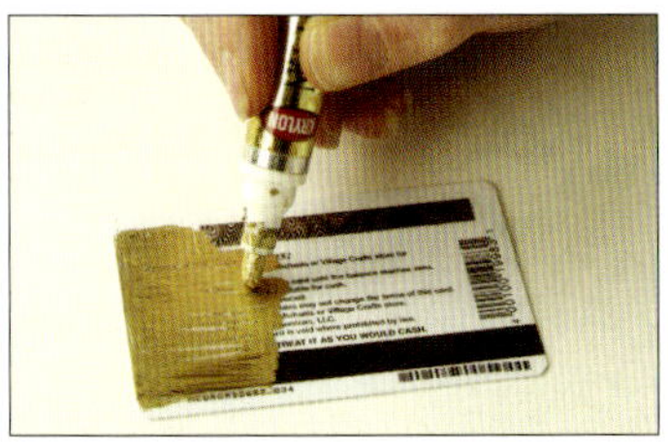
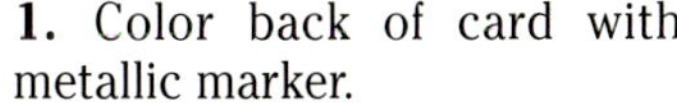

1. Color back of card with metallic marker.

2. Mark strips on front of card.

3. Cut strips.

4. Remove marker with cleaner.

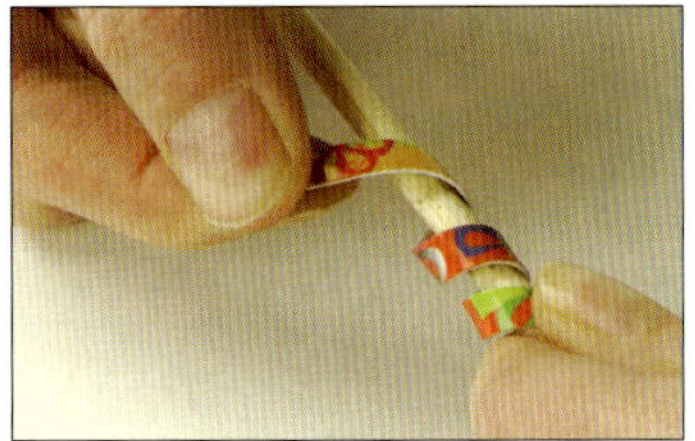

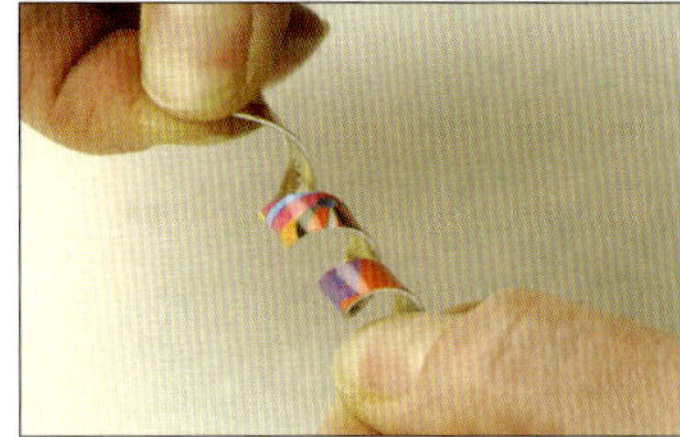

5. Punch hole in one end of each strip.

6. Wrap each strip around a dowel rod.

7. Shape ends with pliers.

8. Stretch spiral to lengthen it.

The Frosty Snowman Pendant

by Andrea Gibson

Turn a holly jolly snowman gift card into a cheerful seasonal pendant.

SIZE: 2 1/8" x 2 3/4"

MATERIALS:

2 gift cards (Green, Blue) • Silver non-tarnish 20 gauge wire, 3 spiral dangles • Jump rings (6 medium, 2 large) • 30 Blue seed beads • Snowflake charm • 3 tiny Lime Green brads • 3 photo anchors (Green, Blue, White) • 1 Silver photo hanger • 24" ball chain • 4 head pins • Lime Green bottle cap • Citrus Brights bottle cap stickers • Silver paint pen • Sandpaper block • Die cut machine, Dog Tags smallest die • 1/16" hole punch • GLOO Clear adhesive

INSTRUCTIONS:

Gift Card Preparation: Cut Blue gift card to 2 1/4" square. Round corners. Die cut a small window into left upper corner of Blue gift card. Sand edges smooth. Paint back of card with Silver paint pen. Let dry. Punch holes. Punch 2 holes at top of card using photo hanger as a guide. • From Green card, cut a 3/4" x 1 1/4" piece to fill in behind dog tag window opening. Glue to back of card. Glue Silver photo hanger to back of card. Let dry. Add Green brads.

Bead Loop Dangles: Add Blue seed beads to 4 head pins so that bead strands are multiple lengths. Close with a loop.

Bottle Cap: Flatten Green cap, apply sticker, sand sticker edges. Punch hole in top of cap rim for dangling and 1 hole in cap center for snowflake charm. Attach snowflake charm with Green brad. Dangle from card with large jump ring and 2 medium jump rings. Add 2 wire spiral dangles to jump rings.

Pendant Dangles: First dangle: Attach a Blue photo anchor and a bead strand to card with a medium jump ring.

Second dangle: Attach a White photo anchor, wire spiral dangle, and 2 Blue bead strands to a medium jump ring. Attach to card with large jump ring.

Third dangle: Attach Green photo anchor and a Blue bead strand to card with a medium jump ring.

Finish: Hang pendant from Ball Chain.

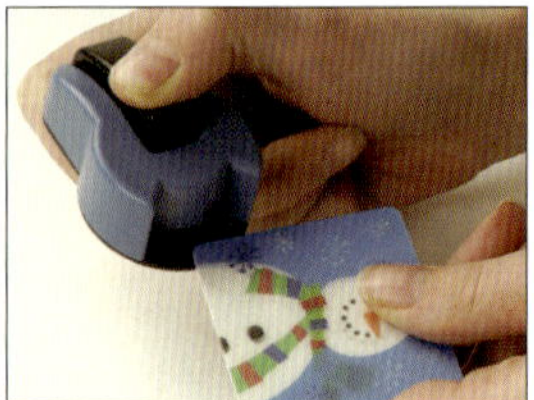

1. Cut out snowman card and round corners.

2. Punch the holes in the bottom.

3. Attach hanger with adhesive and brads.

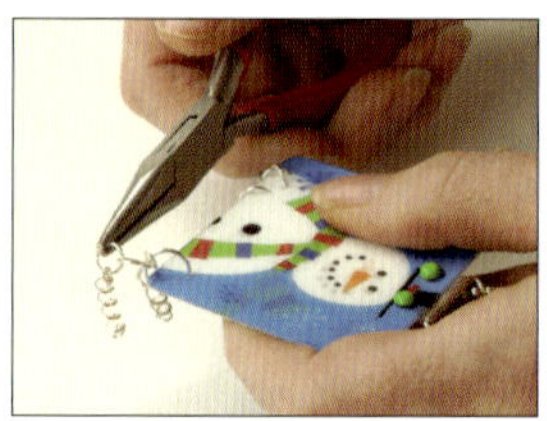

4. Attach dangles with jump rings.

5. Punch out shape and adhere to back.

Heart & Swirl Pin

by Donna Goss

Blazing with hot colors that are so now and a shape that is "tres chic", this pin adds flair to any outfit.

SIZE: 2 1/4" x 3"

MATERIALS:

Gift card • Silver eyelet • Head pin • Jump ring • Beads • Silver paint pen • Silver eyelet and tools • Die cut machine, Dies: Swirl, Heart • 1/8" hole punch • Adhesive

INSTRUCTIONS:

Heart & swirl shapes: Die cut heart and swirl shapes from gift card. Paint edges and back with paint pen. Let dry. Set eyelet.

Bead dangle: Thread beads on head pin. Trim head pin 1/4" from last bead. Make loop in wire and close near last bead.

Pin: Attach bead dangle to swirl with a jump ring. Glue swirl to heart. Let dry. Adhere pin back.

Swirl Pin Pattern

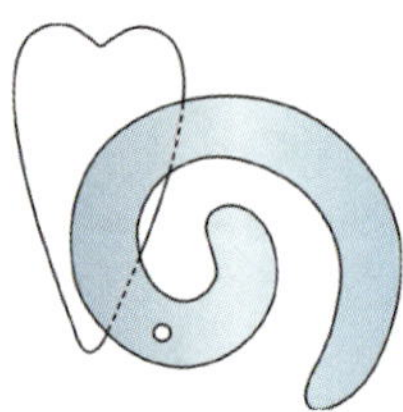

Glue swirl to heart.

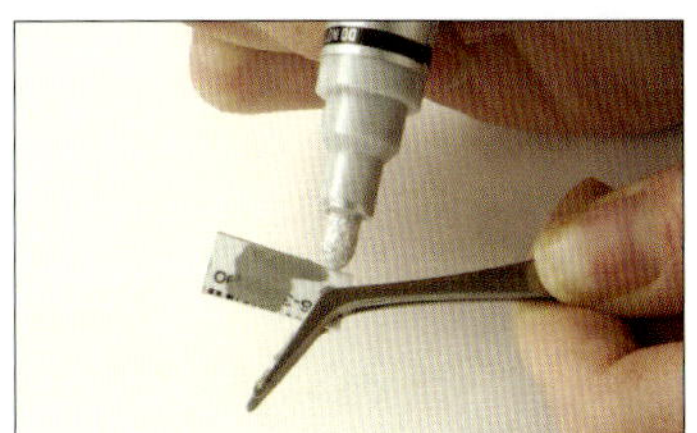

1. Cut and paint back and edges of card pieces.

2. Punch holes and add eyelets.

3. Open jump ring.

4. Make a loop in the wire near the last bead.

Dangle Key Fob

by Donna Goss

Tiny scraps of gift cards become decorative.

SIZE: 4¹/₂"
MATERIALS:
Gift card • Large split ring
• Spoiled rotten soft charm
• 2 Silver eyelets • Head pin
• Silver jump rings • Beads
• Silver paint pen • Eyelet tools
• Tweezers • 1/8" hole punch
INSTRUCTIONS:
Gift Card dangles: Follow instructions for Dangle Bracelet.
Bead dangles: Follow instructions for Dangle Bracelet.
Key fob: Attach gift card and bead dangles to jump ring. Attach jump ring to one end of soft charm. Attach split ring to opposite end of soft charm.

Dangle Key Fob Pattern

Dangle Bracelet and Earrings

by Donna Goss

Tempting turquoise softens shades of green in a sparkling ensemble that captures the essence of water and feels lighter than air.

SIZE: 7¹/₂" bracelet, 2" earrings
MATERIALS:
Gift cards • 7¹/₂" bracelet • Earring loop findings • Silver eyelets • Head pins • Silver jump rings • Beads • Silver paint pen • Eyelet tools • Tweezers • 1/8" hole punch
INSTRUCTIONS:
Gift Card dangles: Cut gift cards into 3/8" x 3/4" rectangles. Punch hole in top of each piece. Use tweezers to hold pieces for painting. Paint edges of each piece first. Let dry. Paint backs. Let dry thoroughly. Set eyelets in holes.
Bead dangles: Thread beads on head pin. Trim head pin 1/4" from last bead. Make a loop in wire and close near last bead.
Bracelet: Attach gift card and bead dangles with jump rings to bracelet.
Earrings: Attach a jump ring to earring loop finding. On another jump ring attach a gift card dangle and a bead dangle. Attach the 2 jump rings together to complete.

Strips A Blazing Necklace

by Andrea Gibson

Classy and eclectic, colorful strips are destined to become your favorite accessory.

SIZE: 20"

MATERIALS:

Gift card • 5 square Antique Silver spacers • 11 round Red beads • 12 large cast metal Silver #3 spacers • 9 small round Czech glass Jet Black beads • 9 small round Silver Diamond Daisy spacers • 20" Black leather cord • 2 Silver coil ends • 1 Lobster Claw 14mm clasp • Silver non-tarnish 20 gauge wire • Silver medium jump ring • Black micro glitter • Silver paint pen • Sanding block • 1/16" hole punch • Glossy Accents

INSTRUCTIONS:

Gift Card Preparation: Cut card into six 1/4" strips. Punch hole in top of each strip. Cut strip bottoms diagonally at different lengths. Sand edges smooth. Paint back and edges of each strip with Silver paint pen. Glaze and sprinkle diagonal cut with Black glitter. Let dry.

Bead Wraps: Cut nine 3" pieces of Silver wire. Make 5 bead wraps: Make a loop in one end of wire, load small round Silver spacer, Black round bead, round Red bead, square Silver spacer. Close with bead wrap technique. Make 4 as above without square Silver spacers. • Cut two 2" pieces of Silver wire. Make 2 bead wraps with 1 Red bead. Close with bead wrap technique.

S-Hooks: Make 17 S-hooks using 20 gauge Silver wire. Attach to one end of each bead wrap and card strip. Close S-hooks.

Necklace Assembly: Attach coil end with jump ring to one end of Black leather cord. Load beads through S-hook onto leather: 1 small bead wrap, 2 medium bead wraps, Silver spacer, card strip, spacer, large bead wrap, spacer, card strip, spacer, etc. Complete necklace with coil end, medium jump ring and lobster claw clasp.

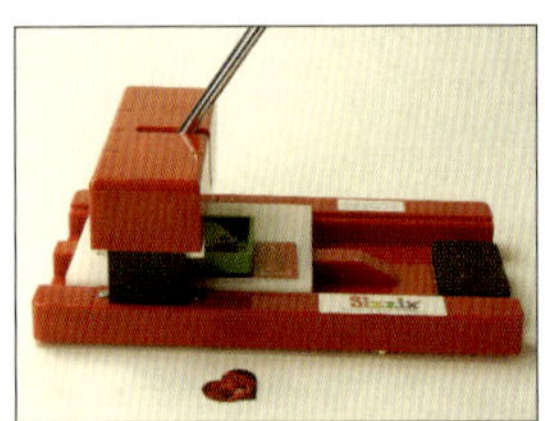

1. Die cut heart shapes.

2. Sand heart edges.

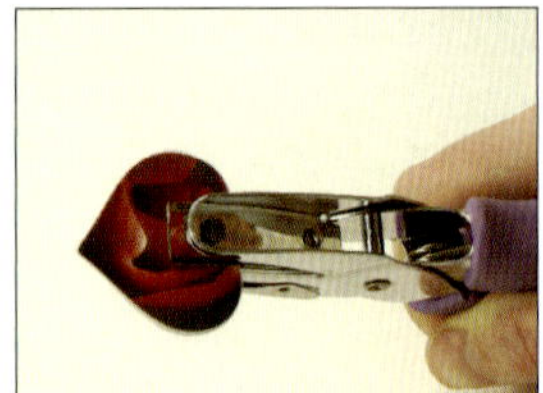

3. Punch a hole in the top of heart.

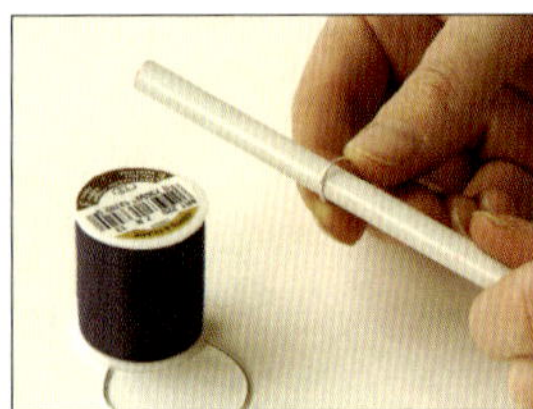

4. Shape wire.

5. String hearts and charms on wire.

6. Turn loops in shaped wire ends.

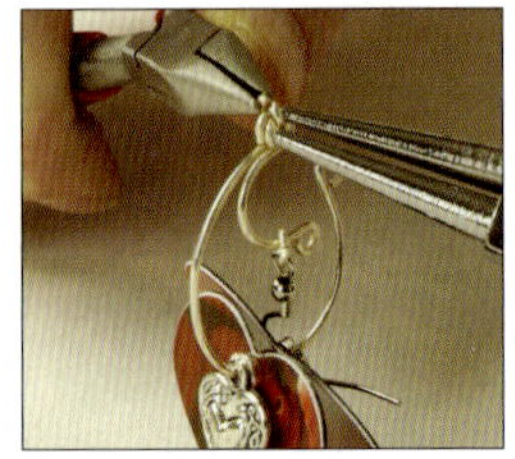

7. Attach top wire with jump rings.

Dangling Hearts Earrings

by Andrea Gibson

Make sumptuous earrings this afternoon and wear them tonight!

Tip: Extra sanding makes beautiful White edges on the hearts.

SIZE: 1 1/2"

MATERIALS:

2 gift cards • Earring wires • 2 heart charms • 8 flat Silver spacer beads • Silver non-tarnish 18 gauge wire • *Krylon* Black fusion for plastic spray paint • Sanding block • Small thread spool • Die cut machine, Hearts die: 2 smallest patterns • 1/16" hole punch

INSTRUCTIONS:

Gift Card Preparation: Spray paint the back of 2 cards. Let dry. From each gift card, die cut 1 small and 1 medium heart. Sand heart edges until smooth. Pierce a hole in each heart top center.

Wire earring: Bend two 3" pieces of Silver wire around a small thread spool making a semi circle. Form a loop in one end, turning out. Load Silver spacer, large heart, 2 Silver spacers, small heart, Silver spacer and heart charm. Form loop to match other end. Bend two 1 1/2" pieces of Silver wire around pencil or dowel, making a semicircle. Put a loop in each end, turning out. Connect the semi circles with small jump rings. Add a small jump ring to top semicircle. Add earring wire.

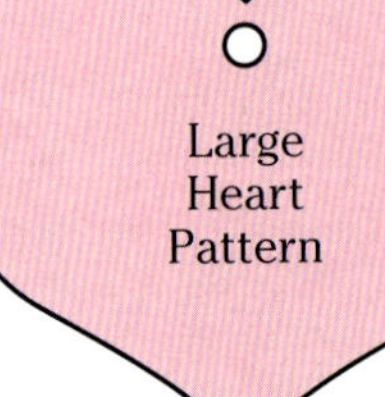

Long Strips Bracelet

by Michele Charles

Sensual red and opulent gold lend exquisite style to a bracelet that is incredibly comfortable to wear.

SIZE: 8"

MATERIALS:

Gift card • 8" Gold chain bracelet • 7 Gold lantern spacer beads • 7 Red cube beads • Gold seed beads • Gold head pins • Gold jump rings (3mm, 5mm) • 1/16" hole punch • Gold metallic paint pen • Glossy Accents

INSTRUCTIONS:

Gift Card Preparation: Cut card into 8 strips 5/16" x 1". Paint back and sides. Let dry. • Punch holes. Paint with Glossy Accents. Let dry.

Bracelet: Attach strips to bracelet with jump rings.

Bead Dangles: Thread Gold seed bead, Red cube bead, Gold seed bead, Gold lantern, Gold seed bead. Make a wrapped loop at the top of a head pin. Attach to bracelet with jump rings.

Heart Purse Pin

by Andrea Gibson

Are you passionate about accessories? You won't be able to resist this red hot purse pin.

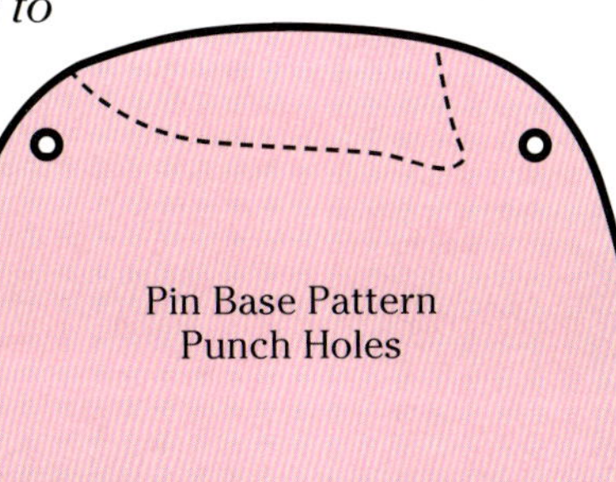

SIZE: 2 1/4" x 2 1/2"

MATERIALS:

Gift card • Small Black rhinestone • Silver spacers (4 diamonds, 1 small round daisy, 1 tiny dragonfly) • 8 Red seed beads • 2 decorative head pins • Silver non-tarnish 18 gauge wire • Silver paint pen • Sanding block • Nylon jaw pliers • 1/16" hole punch • Glossy Accents • GLOO Clear adhesive

INSTRUCTIONS:

Card Preparation: Cut out Purse and Heart following patterns. Sand edges. Paint back of each piece with Silver marker. Glue purse pieces together. Let dry.

Wire Purse Details: Cut 3" of wire. Turn a small loose swirl in each end of the wire. Bend in the middle forming a "v". Cut 1" of wire. Make an S-Swirl, turning a loose swirl in both ends of wire in different directions. Glaze. Add purse details while glaze is wet. Let dry. Punch 2 holes for wire purse handles. See pattern. Cut out credit card logo, sand edges, punch hole in top. Add jump ring, dangle from handle.

Purse Handle: Cut 6" of wire. Bend to form handle. Add 4 spacer beads. Bend a right angle into handle towards ends. Thread each end through to back of purse. Turn a loop on both sides to hold handle in place on purse. Flatten handle down and close wire tightly with nylon jaw pliers.

Loop Bead Unit: Load seed beads and a spacer on each head pin. Turn loop in top. Attach to purse handle to dangle.

Finish: Adhere pin back in place.

1. Punch holes in purse and thread wire.

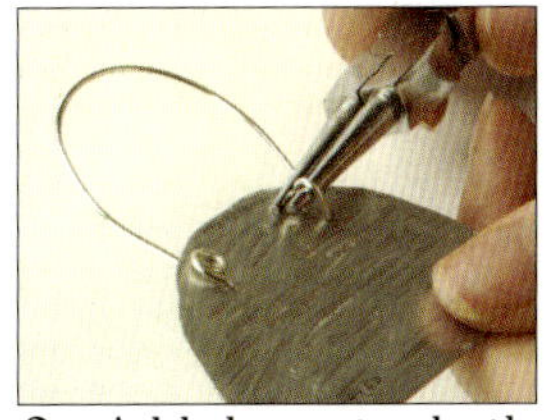

2. Add loop to both sides.

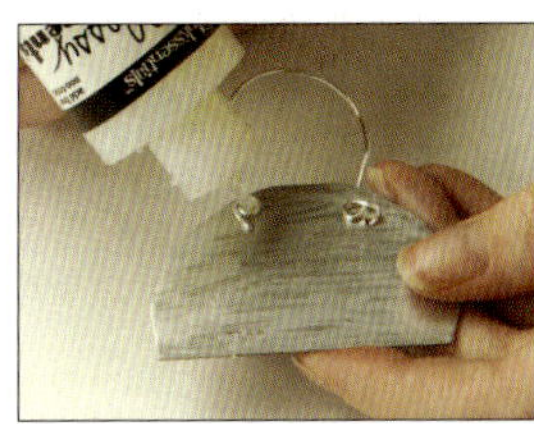

3. Glue ends to back.

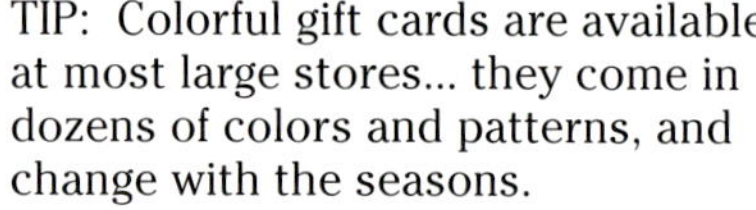

TIP: Colorful gift cards are available at most large stores... they come in dozens of colors and patterns, and change with the seasons.

Shop Till You Drop Bracelet

by Andrea Gibson

Grab your purse. It's time to go shopping. Our Shop Till You Drop bracelet is so much fun to wear you won't want to leave home without it.

MATERIALS:
2 gift cards • 3 old credit cards • 7" Silver charm bracelet • 7 small round Green beads • 7 Aqua round crystals • 7 Diamond Daisy Silver spacers • 7 Silver spacers • Small Black rhinestone • Small Yellow flower brad • 14 Pink glass beads • 7 decorative head pins • 14 Silver head pins • 5 Lobster Claw clasps 14mm • Silver non-tarnish 18 gauge wire, 20 medium 18 gauge jump rings, 3 S-hooks 18 gauge • Aqua Mermaid glitter • Silver paint pen • 1/16" hole punch • Glossy Accents • GLOO Clear adhesive

INSTRUCTIONS:
Gift Card Preparation: Cut logos from credit cards. Sand edges smooth. Punch hole in each logo. Paint back of each logo with Silver marker. Add S-hook to logos. Attach to bracelet, spacing evenly.

Purse charms: Cut out Purse Charms following patterns provided. Sand edges smooth. Paint back of each purse with Silver marker. Glue purse pieces together. Let dry. Glaze. Add purse details while glaze is wet. Let dry. Punch holes for wire purse handles.

Purse handles: Add 2 jump rings and a Lobster Claw clasp to each purse charm. Attach to bracelet, spacing evenly.

Loop Bead Units: Using head pins, make 7 loop bead units with Green beads. Make 7 with 2 Pink beads each and a Silver spacer in the middle. See page 6.

Bead wrap units: Using 7 decorative head pins, make bead units with Aqua round crystals and Silver spacers, then wrap. See instructions at right.

Bracelet: Cluster 1 of each unit together with a medium jump ring. Attach to bracelet, spacing evenly.

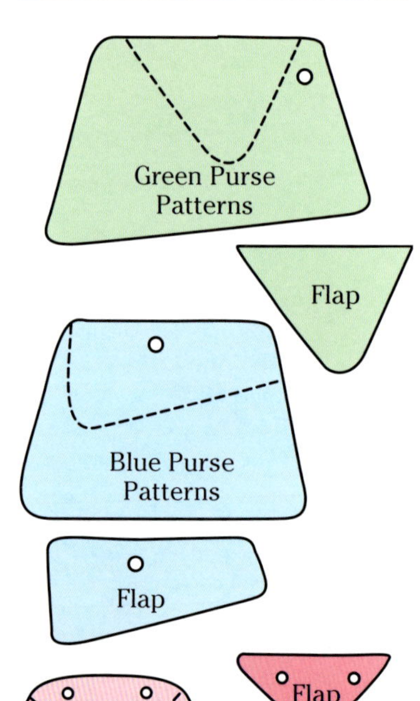

1. Cut out purse shapes and sand edges.

2. Glue purse pieces together. Apply Glossy Accents.

3. Using tweezers, apply the details while glaze is wet.

Making Bead Wrap Units

Thread beads on head pin. Grasp pin with pliers 1/8" from the end of the jaws. Bend wire at a 90° angle. Pivot pliers from horizontal to vertical.

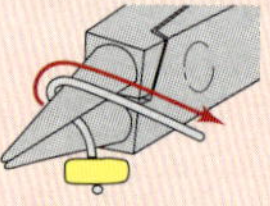
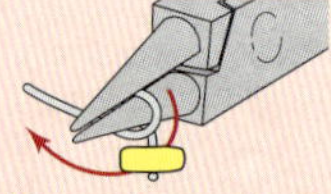

Wrap wire around top jaw of pliers. Reposition wire on bottom jaw of the pliers. Wrap wire around bottom jaw of the pliers.

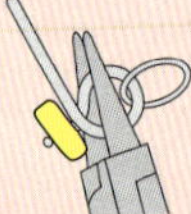
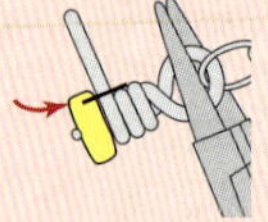

Slip straight end of head pin through the jump ring. Grasp the loop of the dangle with pliers. Without touching the bead, begin coiling the short end around neck of dangle. Begin coils as close to loop as possible. Note: If using plain wire, make a loop at both ends.

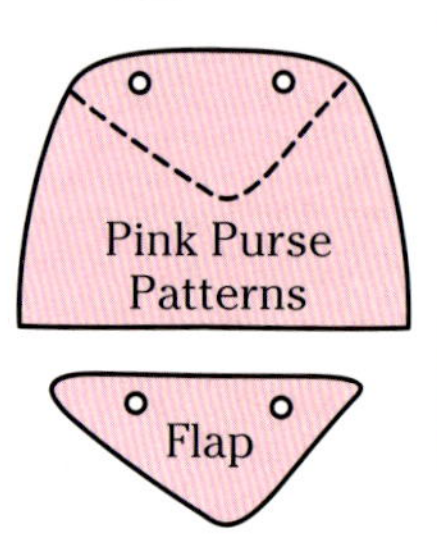

Memory Necklace

by Andrea Gibson

Charm frames bring a touch of nostalgia to this Victorian style locket necklace.

SIZE: 18" - 20"

MATERIALS:

2 gift cards • 18"-20" Silver multi link chain • Toggle clasp • Silver non-tarnish 20 gauge wire, 7 S-hooks • 22 medium jump rings • 3 charm frames • 3 heart charms • Dome initials stickers • 6 Czech glass Red #2 flower beads • 6 Silver spacers • Hematite beads (8 medium, 6 small, 6 tiny) • 6 clear glass bugle beads • Silver paint pen • Sanding block • Punches (1/16" circle, 1" deckle edge square)

INSTRUCTIONS:

Gift Card Preparation: Punch 7 deckle edge squares from 2 gift cards. Lightly sand edges. Punch a hole in the center top of each square. Paint back of squares with Silver marker. Let dry. Add sticker initials.

Loop Bead units: Cut eight 2" pieces of wire. Make 8 loop bead units with medium Black hematite beads. See page 6.

Bead wrap units: Cut six 4" pieces of wire. Make 6 bead wrap units. Load the beads in this order: Red flower, small hematite, Silver spacer, tiny hematite, Clear bugle bead. Finish wrap. See page 16.

Clusters: Make clusters on jump rings: 3 with a Black bead unit and a Silver frame; 3 with a Black bead unit and a Silver heart charm.

Necklace Assembly: Starting in the middle of the Silver chain, attach each square with an S-hook and medium jump ring, spacing squares evenly. The bead units attach to chain in this order: Silver frame unit, Silver heart unit, bead wrap, bead loop, bead wrap, bead loop, bead wrap, Silver frame unit, Silver heart unit, bead loop, bead wrap Silver heart, bead wrap, Silver frame. Finish necklace by adding toggle clasp to end of chain.

1. Use a square deckle punch to cut out card charms.

2. Add charms to chain with jump rings.

Star Key Fob

by Donna Goss

Turn an ordinary key ring into something extraordinary with simple gift tag cut-outs and creative embellishments.

SIZE: 1 1/2" x 3"

MATERIALS:

Gift card • Split ring • Dog tag • Silver star beads • Beads • Pink clipola • Head pin • Jump ring • Die cut machine, Star die • Adhesive

INSTRUCTIONS:

Bead dangle: Thread beads on head pin. Trim head pin 1/4" from last bead. Make loop in wire. Close near last bead.

Tag: Die cut star from gift card. Adhere star, clipola and star beads to tag. Attach bead dangle and tag to jump ring. Attach jump ring to split ring to complete.

Heart Pin

by Donna Goss

Create dangles on a truly charming pin.

SIZE: 2 1/4" x 2 1/4"

MATERIALS: Gift card • Kilt pin • Heart charm • Silver eyelet • Head pin • 3 jump rings • Beads • Silver paint pen • Eyelet tools • *Sizzix* (Die cut machine, Heart die) • 1/8" hole punch

INSTRUCTIONS:

Heart shape: Die cut heart shape from gift card. Paint edges and back with Silver pen. Let dry. Punch hole near top of heart. Set eyelet in top near point.

Bead dangle: Thread beads on head pin. Trim head pin 1/4" from last bead. Make loop in wire and close near last bead.

Pin: Attach charm, gift card heart and bead dangle with jump rings to kilt pin.

Blue Dots Bracelet and Earrings
by Michele Charles

Fishing lures never looked so beautiful. This delicate gold bracelet is made from - who'd have thought it - fishing lures!

MATERIALS:

Gift card • Beads (Turquoise Silver lined E, Red seed) • 9 tiny rhinestones • Eyelets • Eight 3-prong fishing swivels • Gold toggle clasp • 7 head pins • 2 eye pins • Jump rings (3mm, 5mm) • 2 ear wires • $^1/_{16}$" hole punch • Metallic Gold pen • Eyelet tools • Glossy Accents

INSTRUCTIONS:

Gift Card Preparation: Cut card into $^5/_8$" squares. Paint back and sides with Gold pen. Let dry. • Punch a hole in one corner of each square. Set eyelets in holes. Glue a rhinestone to each square. Paint with Glossy Accents. Let dry.

Bracelet: Attach swivels to each other with jump rings. Attach squares to swivel. Thread head pins with seed bead, E bead, seed bead. Form wrapped loop in end. Attach to each jump ring between swivels. Thread an E bead onto two jump rings and use each one to attach a part of the clasp to the bracelet.

Earrings: Thread beads on eye pins. Make a wire wrap on the end of eye pins. Attach ear wire to wire wrap. Attach gift card square to eye pin.

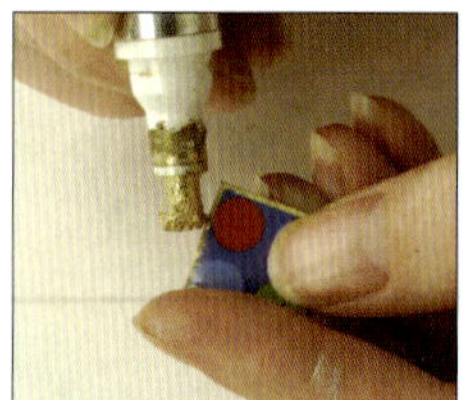

1. Edge squares with gold marker.

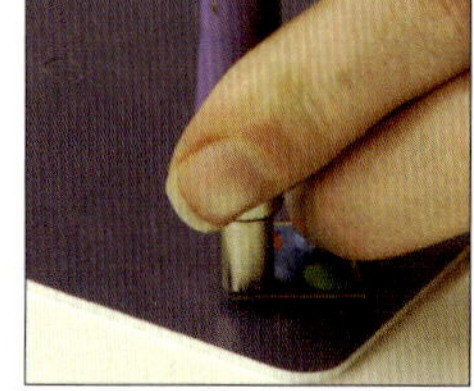

2. Punch holes and set eyelets.

3 Coat squares with Glossy Accents.

4 Add a tiny rhinestone to each square.

Michele Charles

One of the most effervescent, exciting, and effective teachers of multi-media in the industry today is Design Originals' senior educator, Michele Charles. Michele travels across the country bringing her energetic presentation style and sense of humor to workshops that are loaded with innovative techniques.

Her classes are fun-filled excursions designed to ignite the creativity of everyone that attends. This versatile artist develops fresh project ideas for jewelry, rubber stamping, cardmaking, scrapbooking, altered art, trading cards, calligraphy, and polymer clay.

For more information, visit Michele's website at www.michelecharles.com

Andrea Gibson

"I love to make things with my hands and share my creativity with others. I became a certified craftaholic 8 years ago when I began scrapbooking. I love to learn and teach new ideas."

Andrea currently designs layouts, cards and jewelry. She instructs for Artistic Wire. You will also find her work in PaperCrafts, Rubber Stamper, Scrapbook Etc., Paperkuts, Scrapbook Retailer, and books by Design Originals.

You can contact Andrea at andreagibson@earthlink.net.

Donna Goss

Donna is fascinated with jewelry. "While experimenting with gift card jewelry, I found the bright colors tantalizing and I love working with new materials."

Donna has created stamp art since 1992. Her talents includes soldering, collage, scrapbooking and metalwork.

Well known for her quarterly Creative Card class at Stamp Asylum in Plano, Texas, she continues to master all kinds of mixed media.

You can contact Donna at donnagoss@verizon.net

SUPPLIERS - Most craft and variety stores carry an excellent assortment of supplies. If you need something special, ask your local store to contact the following companies:

MARKERS & PAINT - Krylon, Marvy Uchida
ADHESIVES - Aleenes, Crafters Pick, KI Memories
PUNCHES - McGill
RUBBER STAMPS - Hero Arts, Limited Edition, Postmodern Design, Savvy, Stamp in the Hand

WIRE - Artistic Wire
STAZ-ON INK - Tsukineko
GLOSSY ACCENTS - Ranger
DIE-CUTS - Sizzix

MANY THANKS to my friends for their cheerful help and wonderful ideas!
Kathy McMillan • Suzin Hines • Patty Williams
Diana McMillan • Donna Kinsey • David & Donna Thomason